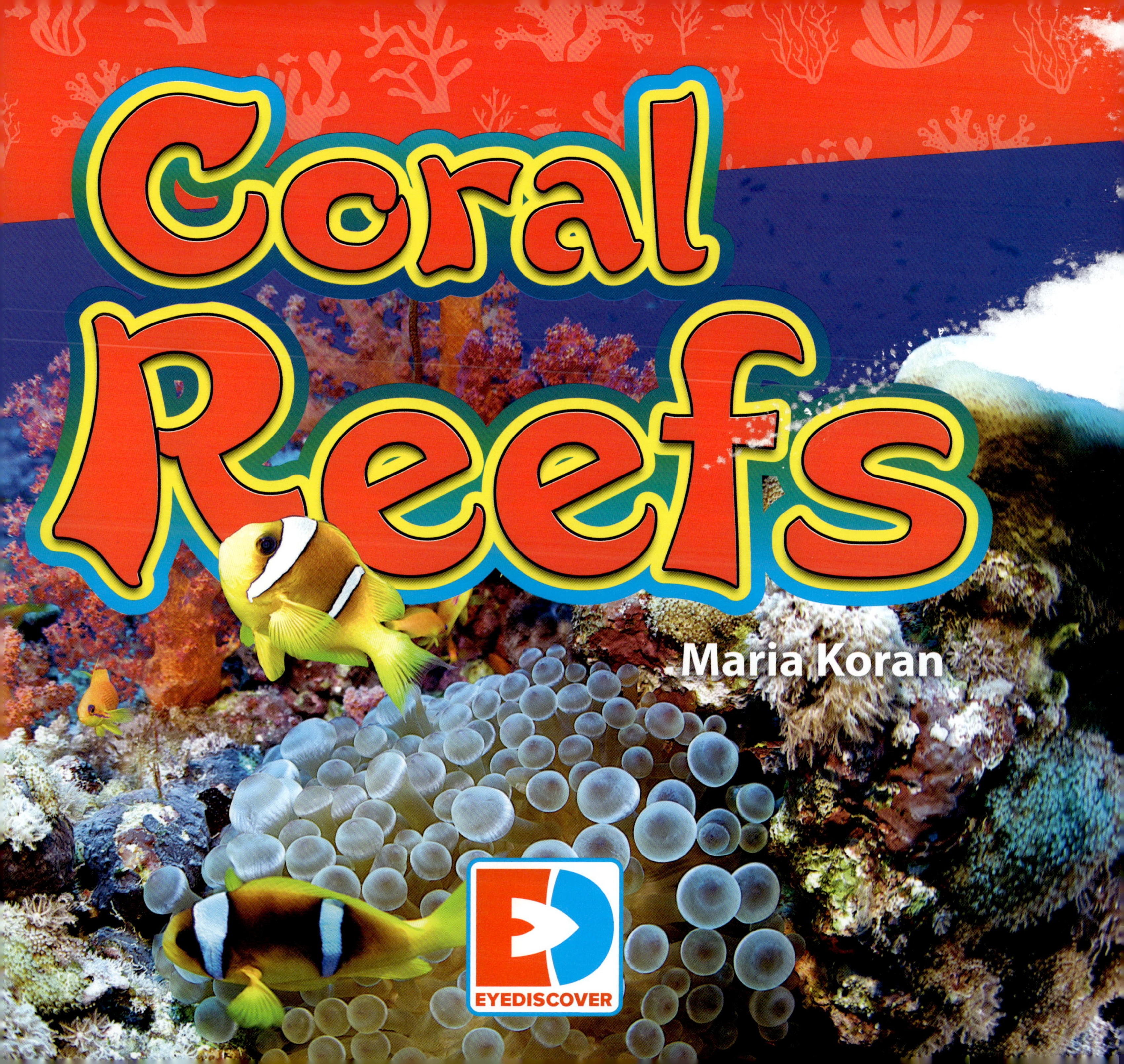
Coral Reefs
Maria Koran
EYEDISCOVER

Go to **www.eyediscover.com** and enter this book's unique code.

**BOOK CODE**

**AVQ92497**

**EYEDISCOVER** brings you optic readalongs that support active learning.

Published by AV² by Weigl
350 5th Avenue, 59th Floor New York, NY 10118
Website: www.eyediscover.com



Library of Congress Cataloging-in-Publication Data available on request

ISBN 978-1-7911-0804-5 (hardcover)

Printed in Guangzhou, China
1 2 3 4 5 6 7 8 9 0 23 22 21 20 19

072019
121818

Project Coordinator: John Willis
Designer: Mandy Christiansen and Ana María Vidal

Weigl acknowledges Getty Images, iStock, Minden Pictures, and Shutterstock as the primary image suppliers for this title.

EYEDISCOVER provides enriched content, optimized for tablet use, that supplements and complements this book. EYEDISCOVER books strive to create inspired learning and engage young minds in a total learning experience.

**Watch**
Video content brings each page to life.

**Browse**
Thumbnails make navigation simple.

**Read**
Follow along with text on the screen.

**Listen**
Hear each page read aloud.

## Your EYEDISCOVER Optic Readalongs come alive with...

**Audio**
Listen to the entire book read aloud.

**Video**
High resolution videos turn each spread into an optic readalong.

**OPTIMIZED FOR**
- ✓ TABLETS
- ✓ WHITEBOARDS
- ✓ COMPUTERS
- ✓ AND MUCH MORE!

In this book, you will learn about

- what they are
- where they are
- what lives there

and much more!

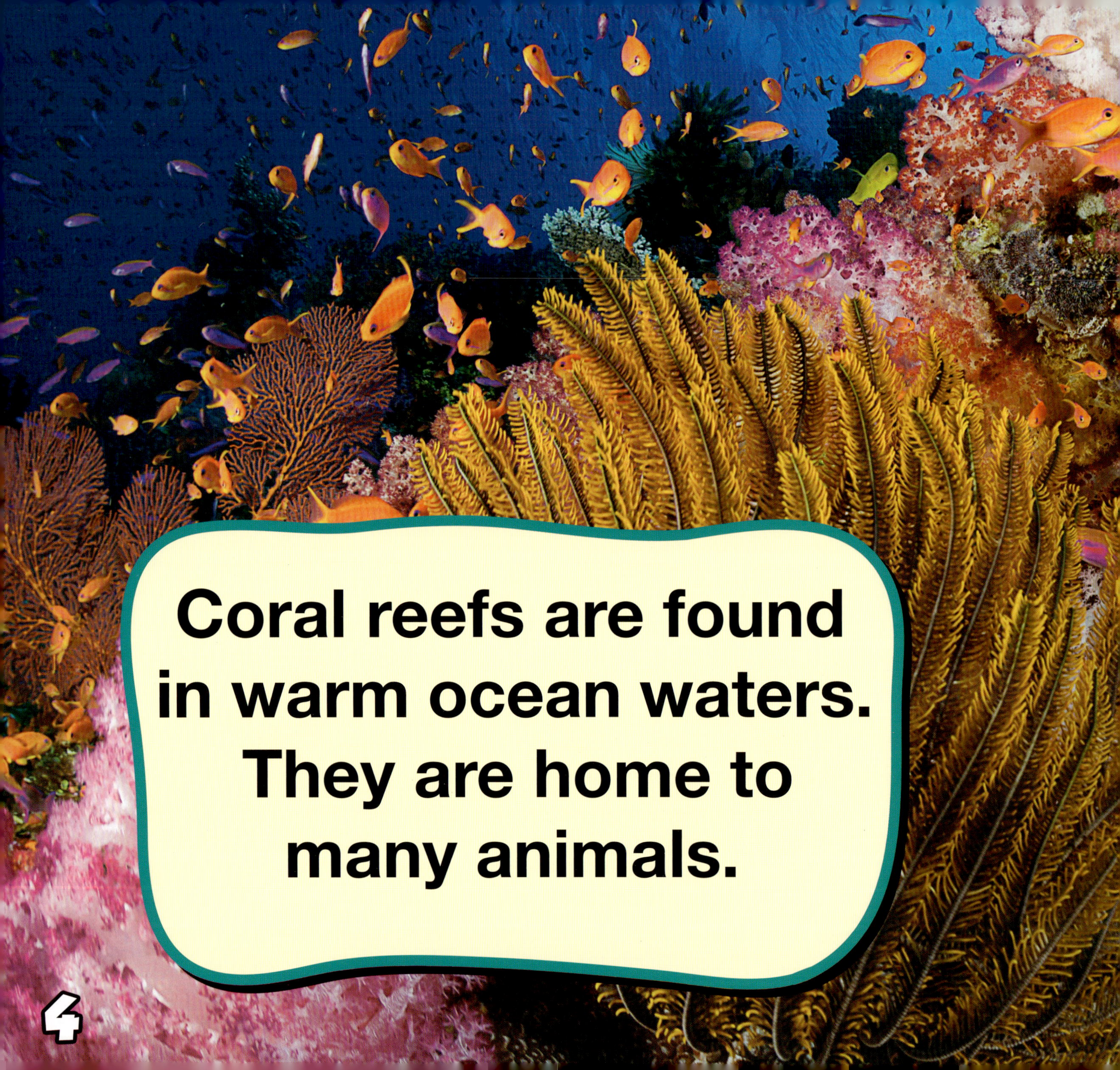

Coral reefs are found in warm ocean waters. They are home to many animals.

Sharks, turtles, and colorful fish can all be found in coral reefs.

Coral reefs are made by tiny animals. They are called coral polyps.

Coral polyps make hard skeletons. Other animals live in these skeletons.

Coral reefs get their color from tiny algae. Algae are living things that make food from sunlight.

The Great Barrier Reef is in Australia. It is the largest coral reef on Earth.

Many people visit coral reefs. They can watch the animals living in the coral.

People should swim above coral reefs. Touching coral can hurt it.

Garbage in water can hurt coral. It is important to keep reefs safe by keeping the oceans clean.

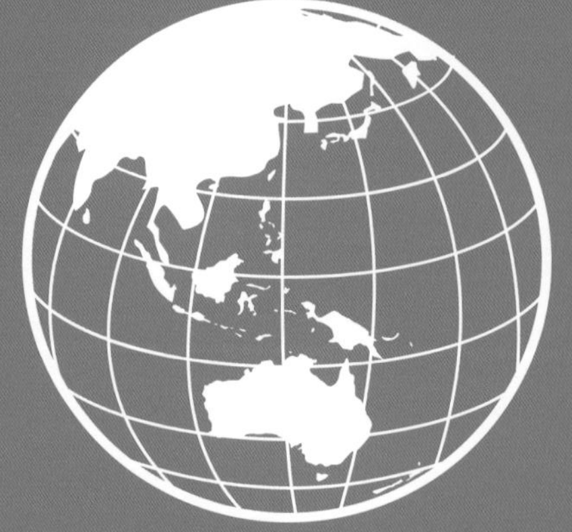

**Coral reefs** form less than **1 percent** of Earth's surface.

**Coral reefs** are home to about **25 percent** of marine animals.

**Most corals** grow less than **1 inch** each year. (2.5 centimeters)

More than 1,500 kinds of fish live in the Great Barrier Reef.

Coral reefs are found in shallow waters of less than 150 feet. (46 meters)

The Great Barrier Reef covers an area of 135,000 square miles. (350,000 square km)

# KEY WORDS

Research has shown that as much as 65 percent of all written material published in English is made up of 300 words. These 300 words cannot be taught using pictures or learned by sounding them out. They must be recognized by sight. This book contains 37 common sight words to help young readers improve their reading fluency and comprehension. This book also teaches young readers several important content words, such as proper nouns. These words are paired with pictures to aid in learning and improve understanding.

| Page | Sight Words First Appearance |
|---|---|
| 4 | animals, are, found, home, in, many, they, to, waters |
| 7 | all, and, be, can |
| 8 | by, made |
| 11 | hard, live, make, other, these |
| 12 | food, from, get, that, their, things |
| 15 | Earth, is, it, on, the |
| 16 | people, watch |
| 19 | above, should |
| 21 | important, keep |

| Page | Content Words First Appearance |
|---|---|
| 4 | coral reefs |
| 7 | fish, sharks, turtles |
| 8 | coral polyps |
| 11 | skeletons |
| 12 | algae, sunlight |
| 15 | Australia, Great Barrier Reef |
| 21 | oceans |

**Watch**
Video content brings each page to life.

**Browse**
Thumbnails make navigation simple.

**Read**
Follow along with text on the screen.

**Listen**
Hear each page read aloud.

**Go to www.eyediscover.com and enter this book's unique code.**

**BOOK CODE**

AVQ92497